HEART SHARDS AND LIP BALM

100 self-care poems & affirmative
notes for your journey

IMANI SHOLA

ISBN: 1544241577
ISBN 13: 9781544241579
Library of Congress Control Number: 2017903780
CreateSpace Independent Publishing Platform
North Charleston, South Carolina

to my First Love, and to Mum and Pops.

for hearts that desire(d) simply to be loved as they love(d);
may these self-love poems be most eloquent
when words fail you.

this book is here to love on you
when you're finding it hard to love yourself.

—— *Imani Shola*

CONTENTS

PREFACE

If I speak with the tongues of men and of angels, but have not love for others growing out of God's love for me, then I have become only a noisy gong or a clanging cymbal—just an annoying distraction. And if I have the gift of prophecy [...], and understand all mysteries, and possess all knowledge; and if I have all sufficient faith so that I can remove mountains, but do not have love reaching out to others, I am nothing. If I give all my possessions to feed the poor, and if I surrender my body to be burned, but do not have love, it does me no good at all.

Love endures with patience *and* serenity; love is kind *and* thoughtful, and is not jealous *or* envious; love does not brag and is not proud *or* arrogant. It is not rude; it is not self-seeking; it is not provoked, nor overly sensitive and easily angered; it does not take into account a wrong endured. It does not rejoice at injustice, but rejoices with the truth when right and truth prevail. Love bears all things regardless of what comes, believes all things looking for the best in each one, hopes all things remaining steadfast during difficult times, and endures all things without weakening. Love never fails; it never fades nor ends. But as for prophecies, they will pass away; as for tongues, they will cease; as for the gift of special knowledge, it will pass away. For we know in part and we prophesy in part, for our knowledge is fragmentary and incomplete. But when that which is complete *and* perfect comes, that which is incomplete *and* partial will pass away.

When I was a child, I talked like a child, I thought like a child, I reasoned like a child; when I became a man, I did away with childish things. For now, in this time of imperfection, we see in a mirror dimly a blurred reflection—a riddle, an enigma—but then, when the time of perfection comes, we will see reality face to face. Now I know in part, just in fragments, but then I will know fully, just as I have been fully known by God. And now there remain: faith (abiding trust in God and His promises), hope (confident expectation of eternal salvation), love (unselfish love for others growing out of God's love for me)—these three (the choicest graces); but the greatest of these is love.

(1 Corinthians 13:1-13. Amplified Bible.)

HEART SHARDS AND LIP BALM

PART ONE:
SHARDS
(PAIN)

i do not know who
made your heart hard.
who caused it bit by bit by bit

to
    shatter
        to shards
            of matter like this,

    that
      hardly
          mattered to
              them in their bliss.

                            i do not know
                    who, but
            i do know
        you.

— #1a view from the shard

you loved and hurt hard, Heart-Hard.
cared, now scarred,
but time is healing; healing, yours.

you are scared to love again
but *scared* is *scarred* through
love-shaped glasses.
your heart will heal. i know you feel.
but time is healing as she passes,
and love is real—
a morning star for mourning scars.

i know
your heart's cried heavy rain;
may love's rays warm you soft again.

    — #1b onto the horizon

he hurt you. i know.
and it shattered your world.

but your scars *adorn* you, baby girl.
like gold souvenirs,
that hang from your ears,
of the mountains of tears that you've climbed and those hurricanes conquered.

you were all forged in the fire.
and they, purified gold, complement your tone
alone. now,
          reign with your
          crown,
for you've
          rained and you've
          grown.

forgive him (and thank him for the jewellery.)

— #2 jewels

issues.
tissues
and boxes of them emptied in
tears and fears of and over him.
or the reality of his absence.

who will love me?
where is my example of a man?
your first valentine stood you up.
each since has ended in vain.

baby boo,
love is on her way to you.

               and you will glow.

you.
will.
glow,
from,
the suppressed inner sun that resides in a woman who has finally
felt the warm love of a man

and whose inner girl,
consequently, finally can.

   – #3 daddy

my mum had to be the

man of the house and the wo-
man of the house.

Lord, please let me
only have to be
the woman i am, not the two.
let a man who loves You

come and be my man
and my home's king.

for i am a queen,

and while woman i am,
solely,
woman i am,
wholly.

   – #4 woman

dear man,
it is okay to cry.
to feel.
to peel back your armour and *vulnerable*.

dear mine,
i will be strong for you. you will need me to.

love,
a woman.

— #5 armour

lip balm

i don't trust you.

you hurt me
and then
we were
building the bridge again.
but as

you were lying

the foundations you
were setting our
bridge aflame.

– #6 bridges

please don't you dare
shatter my world and
then try to swan back
in when you

see i've
made a mosaic of
the pieces.

see, i've
made a mosaic of
the pieces.

                      don't you
see? i'm
an heartist.

  – #7 heartwork

it was all that i knew from
young as i grew up,
so i came to the table a love-
filled cup.

but i learnt from quite young that it doesn't
grow on trees
and i learnt through wrong loves that there
aren't many 'me's
when they mocked me and mopped me and
called me naïve.

whenever i sensed and whenever i saw
other cups that were broken i poured. i would pour
and i poured and i poured and some more and some
more.

i was the raincloud, the well and the sea—
the whatever it was they demanded of me—
the watering can, the water. the fall:

i had loved i had poured i had given my all

but you cannot pour out from an empty cup,
or that much love into a broken cup
that just does not want to be fixed,

whose love is unrequited or is mixed.
and some will take your cup of love in haste
and throw it as quickly right back in your face;
forgive them, love onwards, put boundaries in place.

> if you're a cup full of love, don't get taken for a mug,
> *especially* when your capacity is that of a jug.

— #8 the rise

i know your mind hurts.
it is strained, stressed, unrested;
full,
full,
tried and tested.

but as leaves go,
and fall,
fall,
and settle on the ground, just so,
as sound, your mind
will settle
soon.

i   hold you in my prayers;
and   whole you in my heart.

– #9 fall (for those struggling with mental unrest)

i know you are grieving.

take your time.
tears, anger, confusion are all
valid at this time.
mourning: rising and fall-
ing and overcoming then
you're overcome again.
and again and again until your peace comes and rests.
and peace *is* coming. yes,

and she will wipe your messy tears, comb
your hair, air
out the clouded, muffled room
of your mind. and she will be here soon.

i cannot tell you why they left so soon.
but some angels are too precious to remain
in the confines of this world for too long. now their pain
has gone; find joy—for they're rejoicing too,
and you know they want to rejoice with you.

> weeping endures for a night
> but joy comes in the morning, makes
> your tears of sadness smiles of light—

> i'll stay with you, long as it takes.

– #10 mourning

how tragic to spend our
lives neglecting our own
beauty in pursuit of
someone else's charm.

how tragic to spend your
life neglecting your own
beauty in pursuit of
someone else's charm.

— #11 tragedies

i have seen the generation before
struggle.
mum, dad, nan. immigrant and
first generation hustle.
privileged, i was *raised* in this urban bustle
so i am determined to make the end of our journey
eternally brighter than its beginning.

your struggle was not in vain.
we're finding purpose to end your pain.

    — #12 generation observation one

today she told me
what they did to her.
close friends for years
and yet only in tears
today did she open up.

and i saw it again.
i saw in one look.
i saw why i write
and am writing this book.

i asked her what i should
tell the world of girls
and boys and men and women
abused and recovering—or covering.

> when did you begin to believe the lie
> that the way they are treating you is okay?
> that you deserve it? that what they took from
> you
> you cannot reclaim?

> do the opposite, she says.
> they say don't tell? tell. anyone with ears.
> and if no one has ears,
> or you're crippled by fears

then there's what you are telling yourself.
no: your innocence *is* still yours—and for as
long as you claim it.

this *will* be over soon.
all of your healing, wounds still
raw and sore.

me, i am thinking of you,
knowing that one day soon you'll
roar and soar.

– #13 thinking of you

PART TWO:
HEART
(REFLECTION)

take this mistreatment—
this, your kindness being taken for weakness—
as a lesson in what never to let
anyone else have reason to say
was the way you treated them.

— #14 *blessures* as blessings

i have had dark days, too.
i have found that the darkest of days
lead to the brightest of new beginnings.
and *anyone* can have a new beginning.
light is most dazzling in or after darkest darkness.
so stars and sunrises steal our breath.

remain strong. remain strong. your sunrise will *not* be long.
what you are facing is a season, and seasons *always* pass.

— #15 for you, in your dark season

lip balm

beautiful woman,
you settle for love interests
who cannot love on you the way
you merit it. you merit it. but you
settle like a petal in the mud. boo,
do not settle for lovers whose
only gifts to you are time
and space to ques-
tion your value.
unpetal
you.

dust off your
crown and re-place it.
find the path to your
throne and retrace it,
seize the fears of
'aloneness' and chase them
away. then excuse
empty lovers. replace them.

– #16 petals

the soft heart loves hard
the hard heart's hardly-love,
because it's learnt the hard art of loving itself.

   – #17 h *e* art = hard *et* art

hold me in your loving sentences and nurture me.

read between the lines of all my inner poetry.

trace my quavers and my quivers, musicality.

listen to my questions. question them with me.

love my naked weaknesses and all of my unpleasant.

love between the strands of how my past has reached my present.

try to trace the dots of why i love the way i do.

then and then alone can my heart home herself in you.

   – #18 intimacy

take my hand,
sit me down, and
fall me in love with your mind.
let me write you how i think.
talk me through you; i'll unwind
to you until we're on the brink.

i don't want your words to bounce along the slope of my behind.
i want your words to whisper me the beauty of my mind.

— #19 making (me) love

people respect your boundaries
as much as they respect you.

— #20 boundaries, part one

9/18/17

if you're the one who's always *too nice*
and whose love is taken for granted,
boundaries will save you heartache.
not everyone can partake
in your unhindered love.
limits, boundaries, and standards are the
infrastructures of self-care.

rest there.
say, *this is how far i am going to let you in and no further.*

– #21 boundaries, part two

protect your peace.
if it doesn't sit right with your spirit,
don't pursue it.

nothing in this life is worth exchanging for your peace.

— #22 most precious thing

you've worked too hard,
you're worth too much,
and your future is too bright
to let someone haphazardly become it all.
do not fall
for silk-smooth words and charming flair.
set your standards, discern intentions, love wholly,
care with care.

   – #23 with care, part one

trust your instincts.
if you're sensing someone's heart towards you
isn't pure, you're probably right.
take flight.

detox.
detox.
detox.

— #24 instincts

let nothing
and no-one
steal your joy.
you can't be passive about protecting it.
passivity and protection are mutually exclusive.

   – #25 protection

you are worth too much to settle for mixed messages.
hold people accountable for how they are (mis)handling your
energy
(emotional *and* physical)
and time.

people who haven't clocked onto your time's value
ring mixed messages as alarm bells.

don't deaf.

    — #26 time-bomb

some of the greatest lessons you've yet to learn
will only be learned once you've let go
of what you're currently clinging to most.

leave it;
let it be.

– #27 let go

it is a lot easier to forgive
when you realise the extent of your own flaws.
when you've hosted them at a dinner party.
uninvited, of course.
seen how engorged
they are. how they've grown since you saw
them last and how many of them poured
through your front door at once.
ugly faces. and all of a sudden, when you see them up close,
it's a little easier to be gracious towards another who is battling
their own.
there's humility in forgiveness.

  — #28 flawed

the world around you is full of broken people.
if not broken, fragile.

handle with care.

– #29 broken

you owe it to yourself to

look around. in a public space.
see that no-one like you has ever walked this earth,
nor ever will. you are unique, beautiful, breathtaking.
your life is your legacy;
walk in your beauty and live it unapologetically.

— #30 here's to you

why don't you
like yourself?
your quirks? your looks? you're wrong:

don't you know
your 'different' is the
best part of your song?

— #31 chorus

whatever season you're currently in, reading this,
you've either just overcome a difficult one—conqueror,
or you're just about to, overcomer.

guess what?

that makes you pretty darn incredible.

i'm raising my glass to you.
to you! to you, and all that you do.
love!

   — #32 my love letter to you

you don't have it all figured out right now,
and that's beautiful.

someone who knew everything
couldn't live.

couldn't fall in love with another person's mystery
or trust because they'd never have to, blindly.

trust requires unknown.
hope withstands unknown.
love treasures unknown.

and what is a life without trust, hope, and love?

— #33 unknowing beauty

don't be discouraged by other people's journeys.
yours is your own;
it always has been, and always will be;
no-one else's is the same,
and yours is beautiful.

focus on shaping
your life,
        not escaping

into someone else's.

— #34 the great escape

it's possible to be
simultaneously present and absent,
to be listening without hearing
to be looking without seeing.

learn to be wholly present in
the moment,
this moment,
each that you're in.

— #35 absent presence

if she or he is playing games with your mind,
leave them behind.

do not welcome their abuses—
and stop making excuses.

you, beautiful soul, are worth so much more
than what you so often have settled for

and still do; than being messed around.
please keep your heart, mind and spaces sound.

— #36 sound

turn on my mind first,
i promise my body will follow.

— #37 all i ask (intellect)

everyone is living striving pursuing
with vacant eyes that say "i know what i am doing"
but we are really all just *trying*
and some are inwardly dying
feeling oceanly blue.
so however you
live, above
all, live love.

   – #38 l(i/o)ve

next time you're commuting or in a crowd,
take a moment to observe the people around you.
look up.
look up. each of us is caught up in his or her own world.

when you apply this observation to your life—
to the people who are being difficult with you at the moment,
to the one who abused your kindness, or still is,
to the one testing your patience,
to the one who disappointed you,
to the one who dislikes you for no reason
and has been putting you down,
you'll see that often it's not so much about you,
but more about them and where they're at (or not at)
in *their* world.

live in love.

   – #39 crowds

your words
make and break

lives
souls
hearts
dreams
love.

the matter of life and death,

use them well and wisely.

— #40 words

authenticity is beautiful.
she is rare.
but look around closely and
she is still there.

— #41 real

your creative ideas
your maybe one days
your but i'm so scareds
your when i have times

the dreams that are so big they scare you
and you repress them and they are straining to
come out of that cage you are hiding them in

and each time they re-pop in-
to your mind you re-press to
the absolute agony of your heart?

live them. invest. teach yourself. research. create. start.
conceive, labour, give birth to them. conception, labour, art.

the world is waiting on you to manifest the gift that
we all know you have.

and we know you have
it because none of *us* do.

so waiting, waiting,
          waiting on you.

  – #42 seeds

PART THREE:
LIP
(RESPONSE AND
REVELATION)

a man who treats you like a side-dish
should *never* be your main.

(just makin' it plain.)

  – #43 plain flower

stop seeking approval
from people
who haven't even
won their own yet.

— #44 approval

you've said it so often that even the *birds*
sing that actions speak louder than eloquent words.

  — #45 from a robin

people can only love you
as they've learned to love themselves.
you cannot issue love
from a store of empty shelves.

— #46 bookstores with plenty of issues

baby girl,
stop settling for lovers who stifle all your magic.

the current one is tragic.

– #47 baby girl

9/20/17

Imani Shola

               intelligence knows how to speak.
emotional   intelligence knows when to silent.

— #48 emotional intelligence

looking for love,
seeking your match
but you're empty.

so they'll match you
and empty, too,
and empty you.

don't (ab)use love as a void filler.
first, seek to be whole,
so you can give you, wholly, to one
who loves you, wholly.

    – #49 whole

when they're trying to keep you in a "you-can't" box,
recycle them. cut off; detox.

    – #50 you with big dreams

"i don't know" is a valid answer,
inscribed in the
Ts & Cs of
your humanness.

employ at your leisure.

— #51 small print

Imani Shola

avoid mediocre.
your mother did not carry you for nine months
for you to *average*.

stop dimming your light;
do not be surprised when
people from your past pop up or pop off

the moment you do.
shine your light
—and bright,
boo.

  − #52 three trimesters

if you want to see how man he is,
observe his friends.
they are his character.

often his eyes, his ears and his thoughts, too.

— #53 man he is

hear actions.
watch words.

    – #54 thank me later.

character speaks volumes.
self-righteousness speaks covers.

   — #55 pharisee library

you are neither obliged to have
everything known
nor to reveal
everything known.
a fool tells everyone all on his mind.

wisdom befriends timely silence.

 – #56 known

writing offers healing.
write your heavy heart.
write your frenzied thoughts.
write your current art
ideas. write your broken dreams.
write your '*sure*'s and '*seems*'.

> writing, writing. writing,
> healing in its wings.
> write your broken heart until it sings.

— #57 becoming literate

know yours, boo.
and don't settle for someone who
can't see it.

know it confidently, too.

they don't have to be perfect,
to fit your ideal mould,
to have it figured out,
to glitter gleaming gold.
but to love your precious value,
they must *see* and know they've scored,
and so never want to lose you
—all this *of their own accord*.

   – #58 worth

when people lose faith in you
and discourage you from living your dreams,
it could be that they are too blinded by their own self-doubts
to understand your vision.
some people cannot understand the things they lack.

how can a man who refuses to see
partake in the joy of your vision?

— #59a your vision,

fifty-nine, fifty-nine, fifty-nine *bee*
in short:
stop engaging with those who can't 'see'.

  — #59b protect it.

"you've changed."
is what some people will say to you when, seeing your growth,
they're reminded of their stagnancy.

keep excelling, boo.

— #60 awks *you* still haven't

set them on your own for how you
will and won't be treated.

make them clear. hold fast to them—
and no, you're not conceited.

share in love—not arrogance—with all potential lovers.
steer clear of belittlers, and compromising others'.

   – #61 standards

journal your journey.
thank me later
when you've made it.

you can make it.
you're already making it.

— #62 when you're not yet where you want to be

you are often a culmination of your friends' characters.
who's in your circle,
and what dark circles
are they putting under your eyes
as they circle *compromise*
around your *intuition*?
bad company corrupts good character.
make changes where necessary.

— #63 circles

decisions made in spite of fear
(of what others think,
of what people will say)
and that make your heart leap
because you know it's your passion
are the ones that'll launch you
out of that comfort zone of yours
and into your greatest season.

right now,
you're still in your comfort zone.

when you prioritise your wellbeing (creativity, peace, passions)
over others' perceptions,
it will cause you to flourish.

you decide:

      fear, or flourish.
fear, or flourish.
           fear, or flourish.
      fear, or flourish.
fear, or flourish.

  – #64 flourish

being gifted at it
doesn't mean you won't have to fight, boo.

in fact
you now have complacency fighting you, too.

 — #65 battle

how you feel and how you look
are often closely intertwined.
look good, feel good. body and mind.

not superficial,
it's about acknowledging that
we live in a world where people's impressions of us count
towards how we feel inside (whether we admit it or not).

external views affect internal view.

so. look good, feel good.
they are closely intertwined.
look good, feel good. body and mind.

   — #66 good looks and all the feels

unlearn,
   consciously,
the art of overthinking
sub- *consciously.*
for your own sanity.
   consciously.
sometimes you've got to
   consciously
decide to
   consciously
take what you're seeing
   consciously
at face value.

 – #67 overthinking

our generation faces an epidemic of anxiety.
i have been there.
panic attacks pills unable to swallow anxious dizzy spells you
can't control palpitations i've been there.
protect your peace.
who or what do you need to cut off?
from whom do you need to distance yourself?
limit and tailor the voices that speak into your life—
millennials, especially,
online shopping for approval—
reduce them to the positive, the uplifting.

— #68 swallows and Amazon

1) you cannot be friends
with someone who wants to
discuss your friendship with everyone but you.

2) you cannot be friends
with someone who wants to *be* you.

3) rumour and noise are the same word in French.

– #69 three rules of friendship

your feelings are valid.
the validity of your feelings is never
proportionate to someone else's capacity to understand them.
express them in love.

  – #70 in your feelings

comparison will steal your joy,
personality,
confidence,
quirks.

stop it.
do not even check.
not even sneakily.
just to see how well she is doing,
where he is going now.
stop it. stop it.

your role and gifts are yours alone.
you're in a class—league—of your own.
they can't do you like you do, boo,
so leave that. rocket. rock it—*you*.

– #71 rocket leaves

how you
        act,
        respond,
        make people feel,
        to Love or to Grudge do you hold as you heal?

when you
        speak
        silence
        violence. pause.
        do you act on result before questioning cause?

how you
        let what you've seen
        shape the words that you say.
        your character *speaks* you as sunlight speaks day.

— #72 character

you, here, reading, are loved.
important.
made uniquely.
and *more* than good enough to do it.

fully, wholly, tremendously capable.

your mind is beautiful.
it is so beautifully different to mine.

you can stop striving now.
you have nothing you must prove, and no cynics worth
impressing.

rest.

best,

xo

– #73 rest

lip balm

you can't walk or think straight if
your eyes are eyeing someone else's life each.

— #74 stay calm, stay sweet & mind your business

i am the queen of spades.
let me share what i learnt the hard way.

take that shovel you
are using with all your
might to
prize open a space
for yourself and a place
for yourself in their
clique-fortress.

too coward to include your
light in their darkness they
refuse to make their house your home,
unwelcome.
the insecure lock doors,
shun suns and the bright lights.
for you would cast light on their shadowy places,
your security would illuminate the fear on their faces.

when you have approached with
a heart full of love and a
mind full of truth that there's
room for us all,
banged your head on their door
until your heart is sore.
when you are tired,

take that shovel you
are using to
prize open a space
for yourself and a place
for yourself in their
clique-fortress
and dig the foundations elsewhere
for *your* palace.
build your palace and fling wide open the doors.

may inclusivity colour your royal parades,
O Queen, King of spades.

   – #75 queen of spades

sometimes,
before God can bless you with a lot,
He's got to part you from a Lot
like Abram.

– #76 Genesis

lip balm

their jealousy of you
is free publicity, boo!
tell them
"keep on talking! spread my gospel!
please and thanking you!"

 — #77 jealousy

be wary of mistreating a creative.
we take pain, process it, and spin it into treasure.
gold-drops of wisdom to heal hearts through our art.

– #78 creative

PART FOUR:
BALM
(HEALING)

you are healing.

healing takes time.
allow yourself the space
to feel, re-feel, and heal
at your own pace.

it's a process.
some days you'll feel invincible;
some days you're right back at square one,
like you'd only just begun.

and that's okay.
you're healing, day by day.

— #79 what healing looks like

for my gentle souls out there:
remember to be kind to yourself.
this thing is not easy.
learning to be assertive while
managing your natural inclination
to love too hard
was never going to be smooth-running
or a breeze.

you're doing well.

few will understand your boundaries,
or why, when and how you implement them.
that's okay. boundaries exist to
protect, not to 'make sense'—
no-one may demand an explanation
of them
of you.

  – #80 soft souls

lip balm

you were conceived in joy
and you came into this world in joy
so you carried joy everywhere you went.

so they called you naïve
and spat on your softness,
took your kindness for weakness
and your heart for gullibility.

so with the names and the spit
and the taking (and no giving)
you have often questioned if you were made
for this world
and its dog-eat-dogs.
then my heart met Bro

ken, face-to-face—
that spirit pervading
souls across the globe—
and she herself is broken.
so during our time in my dark

she confided in me, as some hearts do,
and she told me that our rendezvous
would be why i *was* made for this world: to
write souls from her grip and free her from it, too.

— #81 dear me

your past does not define you
or delimit you.
but your mindset can.

decide, then, your goals,
and live pursuing, chasing, and exploring them.

live. i implore you.

   – #82 live past your past-lived

self-care is the first step towards
loving others wholly and steadfastly.

knowing of your flaws helps with forgiving others fast.
listening to your heart teaches you how and when to trust.
loyalty to self enables loyalty to lovers.
loving your whole self will teach you how to love whole others.

   — #83 self-care

forgiveness is,
pieces
to
peace is:
hurt heart
     to art.

— #84 forgiveness is

calm down, boo.

understand you have nothing to prove.

settle into that truth;

feel your exhaustion lift.

   — #85 weight lifting

sometimes you wake up feeling
fragile, don't you? i know.
not ready to face the world today.

that's okay.

affirm that
you are allowed to feel weak sometimes.
know that
the sun is shining even when you can't see it and
you don't have to carry the weight of the day
on your shoulders.
that was never your job.

your job is to take

one day at a time.
one day at a time.
one day at a time.
to live your best,
so take some time to rest.

   – #86 fragile

surround yourself with people
who add to you.
who build you.
who are smarter than you.
who are wiser than you.
who uplift you.
who treasure you.
who are lovingly honest with you.
who remind you of your ideal future you.
who believe in you.
who nurture you.
who pray for you.
who are positive and optimistic towards you.

then strive to be one of those
people who.

then watch and see *flourish*.

— #87 people who

burnt, my heart.
weeps, but only in part.

weeps whole for souls both lost and heaving,
families grieving, hardly breathing,
seething, seeing red.
hearing 'dead' and bleeding bled.

cowardice never belonged to my city
and our people of faith and no particular faith,
and our colours of race and no particular race,
and our flavours of creed and no particular creed.

so she tears up, torn, bleeds
and then tears up, wells, grieves.

but gladder tears flow,
and rips are re-sewn,
seeing those who save lives
risking all, facing knives
and mad trucks and bad lucks.
children, husbands and wives
in those services *braving* and saving our neighbours—
saving our people, our colours and flavours.

lip balm

so here is to them
and those families grieving.
such courage we honour the most;
a toast.

— #88 toast

learn

to "no"

when your mind, soul, and body

say so.

listen to them, stay tuned-in and aim to be aware.

because your life depends on it.
because?
because
self-care.

— #89 assertiveness

people can't help but to float like a buoy
towards you when you brim with unshakeable joy.
while the haters can't help but to hate and to slate it,
the world just can't help but to appreciate it!

    – #90 joy

be still.
stop worrying about what you cannot control.
worry never solved a thing.
it's solved nothing since the last time you
were reading this.

be still.
anxious for nothing; live in the present, and learn to
prioritise

time to be still.

– #91 stillness

when they're trying to tunnel you in,
take a Eurostar to your Paris
and revel in your light and love.

take in eye-fulls of beauty and
tower in the glory of your difference.

you're dope.
admit it.

you're the real *crème fraîche*,
always were,
and *always* will be.

– #92 paris

dream, build, discern, learn.

— #93 mantra

not everything is worth your energy.
pick your battles;
care with care.

— #94 with care, part two

soil-rich, soft, fertile.
chocolate. sweet, warm, melting when loved on
by your tongue.

stone-smooth, jagged, steadfast.
wood-versatile, branched from an ancient tree.
earth. mother of an endangered species—Blood, Life, Melanin—
home, strong.

my skin absorbs the sun and
makes herself richer, deeper.
yes, she spins wealth from gold rays,
turns surface light to depth.

look beyond my surface light,
into my depths. i'm an ocean.

who are you to tell me
that i am poor,
deficient, when my outmost layer
takes light from our universe and
renders it her
treasure?

kinky, coily, curly:
my personality, and each strand
holds history, every swirly curve, curly swerve.
all my kinky kittitian, my juicy jamaican,
my swirly arawak indian
and the curly caribbean.

i could sing forever! but this page won't do—
and this was taken from wood, too.
see? i am everywhere!
eternally basking in
my melanin.

  — #95 ode to my melanin

i love how Taboo
no longer has its slimy claws on
Struggle.
there was a time when one
would not speak of it.

i am proud to be a millennial.
the struggle has just become our hot topic
of conversation.
our journey, our hustle, the hacks.

so i hold so much hope for our
chosen generation.

our struggle is not in vain.
we're finding purpose within the pain.

— #96 generation observation two

to the helpless homeless person——to the beggar on the street,
the words i've been too coward to say to you when we meet:
no matter how inhuman people passing make you feel,
you are precious, you are loved. i pray from your hurts you'll heal.

– #97 sheltering

if you think your family's weird,
know that everyone else's is, too.
but that gene pool was the perfect mix
to create the wonderful you!

– #98 fam

whatever you're called to do, you're cute enough to do it.

you're actually a very good-looking reader.

(i've slyly been watching you back.)

(i'm not a creepy book... i promise.)

— #99 hello beautiful

there are mornings that call for the
lifting of hands and the
tapping of toes and a
dance to the beat of
the swing in your hips and the
song in your heart of the
shards you've let go, and that
balm sugar-sweet
on your lips that you learnt
how to *blend* for yourself,
for you're learning to heal
and to *mend* for yourself!

and *who cares* if they think that we're bonkers?! *we* dance
for bullets dodged and mountains conquered!

   – #100 lip balm

EPILOGUE

dear you,

lovely to meet you.

i've saved this part until the end because i wanted to share my heart with you first and let her speak on my behalf.

i think people's hearts towards us speak louder than their claims about who they are to us.
you claim you are my "friend", but what's your heart towards me saying?

you and this heart you're reading share an immense thing in common: we're both human, here, now, learning, imperfect. just trying to figure this out and get it right.

my name is imani. i am a twenty-year-old student of life, languages and people. this collection has been my heart on paper. i wrote her out in the hope that yours might hear something, too.

my aim in writing this book has been to facilitate and celebrate healing through words among hearts who've been broken, betrayed or felt disillusioned. when i've been there, i've found that the best healing often comes in soothing words from caring lips: lip balm.

i hope you carry this book around with you as easily as your lip balm—that it soothes, reassures and caresses you and that you'll reapply it when you're dry, irritated or sore.

i pray that its message of self-care will gradually replace those heart shards you've been carrying with you as casually as lip balm since that day your heart was broken into shards, and helps you to process your process from heartache to soothing; from chaos to calm; from Heart Shards to Balm.

if you're feeling unloved: i care about you through this book! i hope its existence has shown you that, and that my actions have spoken as loud as my words.

thank you for reading and loving,

imani shola x
twitter.com/imanishola
instagram.com/imanishola

ABOUT THE AUTHOR

Imani Shola has been hailed as one of the most promising young poets in the United Kingdom. At age fourteen, she was named a Commended Winner of The Poetry Society's Foyle Young Poet of the Year Award, selected from thousands of entries from forty-three countries. An adamant believer in the power of words to bring emotional healing, writing has always been Imani's therapy, and selfless loving, her strength. She is currently studying at the University of Cambridge.

19344400R00076

Printed in Poland
by Amazon Fulfillment
Poland Sp. z o.o., Wrocław